YOU MIGHT BE FROM NEW BRUNSWICK IF...

Michael de Adder

MacIntyre Purcell Publishing Inc.
194 Hospital Rd.
Lunenburg, Nova Scotia
B0J 2C0
(902) 640-3350

www.macintyrepurcell.com
info@macintyrepurcell.com

Printed and bound in Canada.

Library and Archives Canada Cataloguing in Publication

De Adder, Michael, 1967-, author You might be from New Brunswick if... / Michael de Adder.

ISBN 978-1-927097-65-6 (pbk.)

1. New Brunswick--Social life and customs--Caricatures and cartoons. 2. Canadian wit and humor, Pictorial. 3. Comic books, strips, etc. I. Title.

FC2461.3.D42 2014   971.5'1   C2014-904837-8

MacIntyre Purcell Publishing Inc. would like to acknowledge the financial support of the Government of Canada through Department of Canadian Heritage (Canada Book Fund) and the Nova Scotia Department of Tourism, Culture and Heritage.

FOR MOM

FOREWORD

We are unique.

I have a friend who says that if Canadians are a modest people, then New Brunswickers are the quintessential Canadians for we rule by modesty. And I believe he might be right looking at Michael de Adder's quirky and sympathetic views of a region that often blends in with the immense country.

We are different, however, and this difference is often visible in details that might escape us when we compare ourselves — something we should never do for we are unique! — to other regions of this country of ours.

How is it ours? I mean how is it ours more than someone else's. OK. Suppose you walk in the woods, and all of a sudden a tree falls? (Sorry I got sidetracked on another problem. Where was I?)

That, though, really is the question, isn't it? Where are we? Where do we stand? Who are we? What is our persona and how do we translate that question into something funny, nostalgic, comforting, and . . . yes . . . unique? That is the quest that Michael de Adder set for himself. In a humourous way, but nevertheless a way that tells as much if not more than a very serious 500 page essay.

This question of identity is a very serious one but it usually boils down to details that we forget to acknowledge. When recognized, however, we all of a sudden become bigger than our individual selves, glowing with pride and we feel ready to dominate the world.

Details are important, that's where the devil is hiding. So the fact that we have invented the chocolate bar is probably as important as the big ax in Nakawic or the big lobster in Shediac, which always reminds me that we live in a land of giants and that we were born to show the way for we see from far away.

But, coming down to more modest considerations, I would say that Michael's book is a fantastic introduction to living in a land that we appreciate, value, and cherish, and indeed this very well may be the reason why we are so unique.

The talent, the art, the down to earth feeling, and the soulful outlook of this collection is a real testimony to sharing the great adventure of a province, this land and its people, that has greatly contributed to the shaping of Canada, in making it prosperous and, yes — one more time with feeling — unique. Never forget that we were there first!

— *Herménégilde Chiasson*

INTRODUCTION

In 2013, *You Might Be From Nova Scotia* hit the shelves, and before that book was even completed there was talk of a second book about my home province of New Brunswick.

I was born in Moncton, and raised in Riverview, so it would be easy, I thought. At least at first glance.

The problem with writing a book that encompasses what it is like to be from New Brunswick is that there are two very distinct viewpoints – one English and one French. And the differences aren't just linguistic. These are two very different experiences culturally. Hopefully this book includes both.

I couldn't have done it without the help of friends and family, and 12 years of French immersion. In French immersion, you don't just learn a language, you learn a whole other culture. I'd like to thank every French teacher I had, from Grade 1 to Grade 12. My marks may not have proven it at the time, but something did sink in.

I couldn't have done this book without the help of my cousin, Erin Dwyer. Thanks for helping me with the Saint John area and making suggestions.

I'd like to thank Meredith MacKinlay for cleaning up the cover, editing the cartoons, and making the grammar much more gooder.

Thanks also to my two brothers, Paul De Adder and David De Adder, for helping me to remember stuff. Thanks to Natalie Dwyer for honking before crossing a covered bridge.

Thanks to the Friday night dinner gang, and especially to Greg Little for gauging his New Brunswick crew – Mark Ebbett, Janice McNeill, and Vern Curry. (My apologies for not including an old car as a septic tank.)

Thanks to Michelle Thornhill, Eric Thornhill, Amber Lounder, and Eric Lounder for early suggestions. To Wanda Baxter for several unique ideas that nobody would have remembered. To Greg Travis and Michelle Doucet for being the closest of friends. And to Rick Farrer for helping to push a shopping cart.

Thanks to my Grade 12 art teacher, Ken Frost, for encouraging me to pursue a career in art.

And again, a special thanks to Gail, Meaghan, and Bridget. Thank you for letting me spend long hours writing another book.

— *Michael de Adder*

YOU MIGHT BE FROM NEW BRUNSWICK IF...

YOU LIKE TO EAT FERNS.

YOU OR SOMEBODY YOU KNOW WORKS FOR THE IRVINGS.

THE ORIGINAL "BACK TO THE FUTURE" CAR
WAS BUILT IN NEW BRUNSWICK.

YOU HAVE RIDDEN A GIANT LOBSTER.

GROUNDING YOUR BOAT IS A REGULAR OCCURRENCE.

YOU DON'T LIKE
THIS A LOT.

YOU LIKE THIS
A LOT.

YOU CONSIDER
THIS TO BE
← BOTTLED WATER

YOU DON'T
MISS THIS →

13

YOU THINK THERE'S NO SHORE LIKE THE NORTH SHORE
THAT'S FOR SURE.

YOU LIKE A ROOF OVER YOUR HEAD
WHEN CROSSING A BRIDGE.

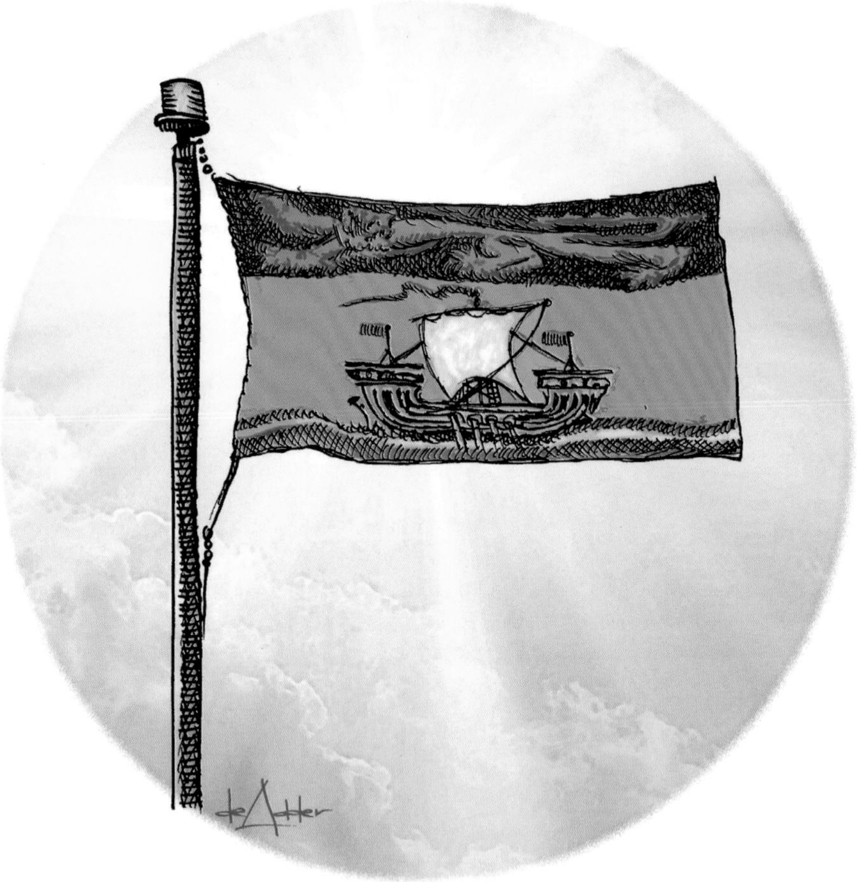
deAdder

THIS MEANS YOU'RE HOME.

THIS ALSO MEANS YOU'RE HOME.

ON JULY 1ST YOU CELEBRATE A NATIONAL DAY.

ON AUGUST 15 YOU CELEBRATE A SECOND NATIONAL DAY.

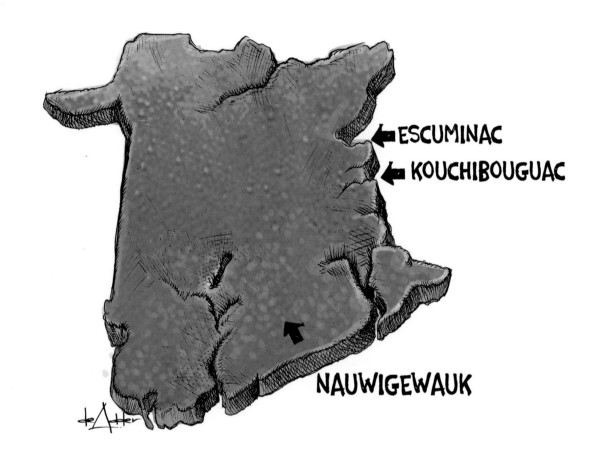

YOU CAN PRONOUNCE KOUCHIBOUGUAC, NAUWIGEWAUK AND ESCUMINAC.

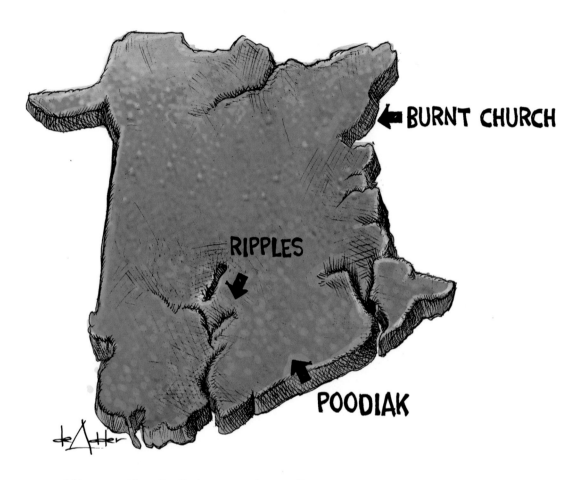

YOU THINK BURNT CHURCH, RIPPLES AND POODIAK ARE NORMAL PLACE NAMES.

YOU HAVE HAD TO SHOVEL OUT YOUR HOUSE.

IN A SNOW STORM YOU REDUCE YOUR SPEED
TO THE POSTED SPEED LIMIT.

YOU HAVE YOUR OWN WAY OF SPEAKING ENGLISH.

YOU HAVE YOUR OWN WAY OF SPEAKING FRENCH.

YOU CAN BUY LOBSTER FROM JUST ABOUT ANYWHERE.

LOBSTER TRAP LAWN ORNAMENT

TIRE PLANTER

WASHING MACHINE DRUM
FIRE PIT

OLD FREEZER
GARBAGE BOX

YOU HAVE YOUR OWN WAY OF RECYCLING.

YOU LOST YOUR MIRROR ON THE OLD GUNNINGSVILLE BRIDGE.

YOU KNOW THIS IS THE BRIDGE
TO CHEAP BEER.

YOU CALL THIS BOOT'NER.

YOU CALL THIS GIV'N'R.

YOU CALL THIS
BEING OUT OF 'ER.

YOU CALL THIS BEING
RIGHT OUT OF 'ER.

YOU KNOW THE SECOND BIGGEST EMPLOYER OF NEW BRUNSWICKERS
BEHIND THE IRVINGS IS ALBERTA.

YOU MISS THE POTATO BREAK.

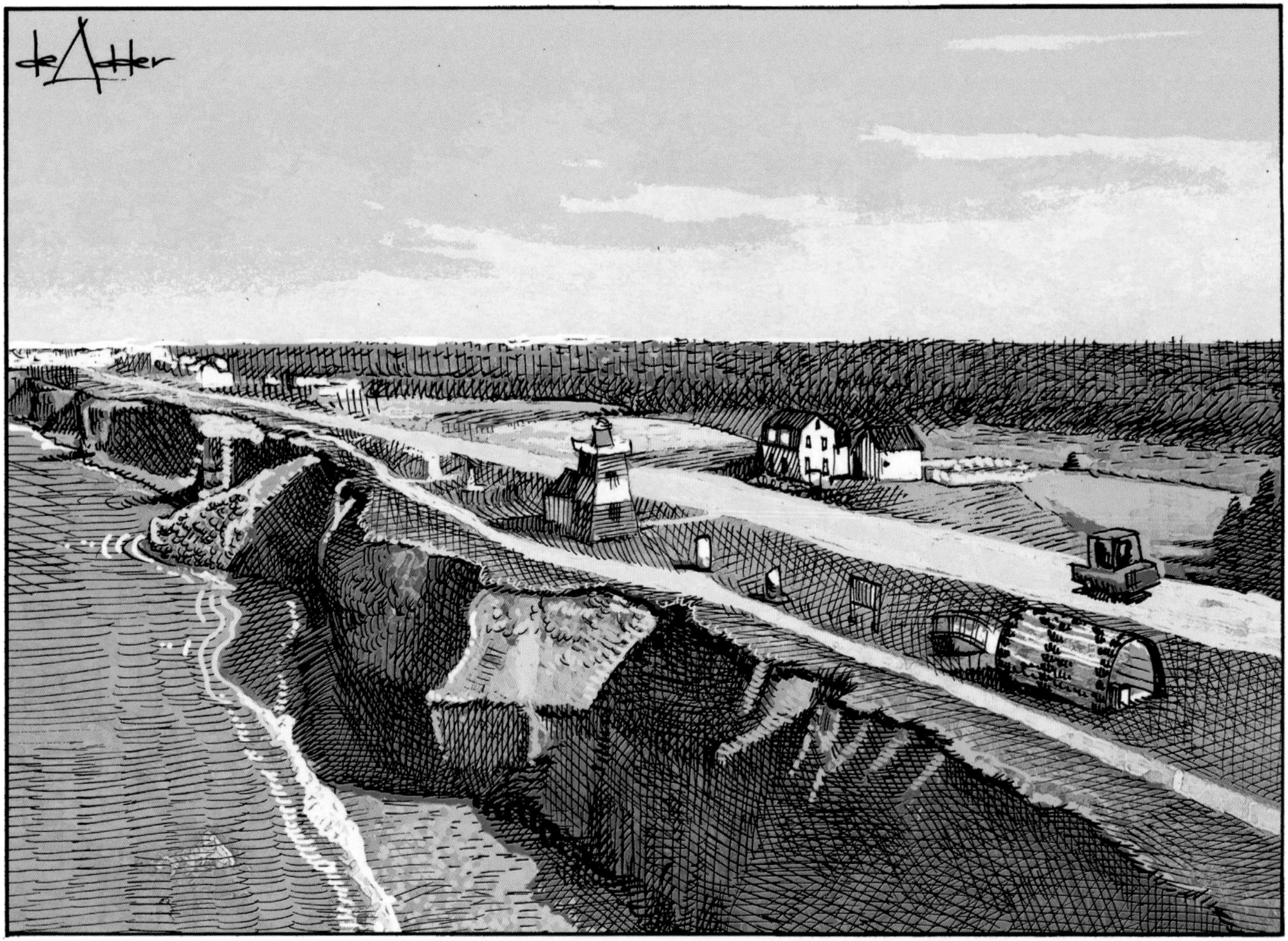
deAdder

YOU KNOW THOSE PEOPLE WHO CALL NEW BRUNSWICK
THE DRIVE-THROUGH PROVINCE, NEVER DROVE ALONG THE COAST.

YOU'VE WALKED ON THE BOTTOM
OF THE OCEAN FLOOR.

SPRING

SUMMER

FALL

INTERMITTENT POWER OUTAGES

THESE ARE NEW BRUNSWICK'S FOUR SEASONS.

YOU KNOW NEW BRUNSWICK IS HOME TO SOME OF THE WORLD'S BIGGEST ATTRACTIONS.

YOU'RE MAD WHEN THE PLOW DOESN'T SHOW UP.

YOU'RE MAD WHEN THE PLOW DOES SHOW UP.

YOU HAVE A UNIQUE RECIPE FOR PANCAKES.

YOU HAVE YOUR OWN WAY OF MAKING STEW.

YOU'VE HAD TO RUN FROM THE TIDE.

YOU'RE STILL NOT SURE IF YOU COASTED UPHILL.

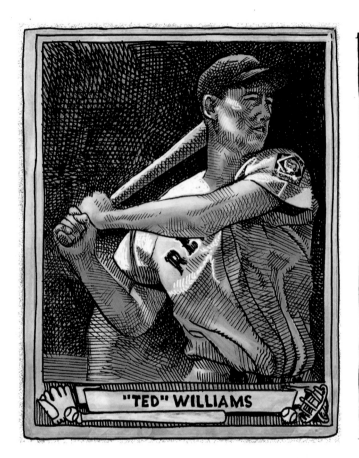

"TED" WILLIAMS

Ted Williams on the Miramichi

YOU KNOW TED WILLIAMS SPENT TIME
FISHING IN NEW BRUNSWICK.

AND BABE RUTH SPENT TIME
HUNTING IN NEW BRUNSWICK.

YOU KNOW FRANKLIN DELANO ROOSEVELT
HAD A COTTAGE IN NEW BRUNSWICK.

YOU KNOW A LIGHTHOUSE YOU CAN WALK TO
ONLY IF THE TIDE IS OUT.

IT DOESN'T FEEL LIKE CHRISTMAS UNTIL YOU'VE HAD YOUR POUTINE RÂPÉE.

YOU CAN STRIP A LOBSTER IN
UNDER THREE MINUTES.

YOU WERE PASSED BY AN ATV ON THE HIGHWAY.

THEN A SNOWMOBILE PASSED THAT SAME ATV.

YOU KNOW THE CHOCOLATE BAR
WAS INVENTED IN NEW BRUNSWICK.

YOU'VE PURCHASED SOMETHING WITH
A HUGE WAD OF CASH.

YOUR CITY HAS AN UPTOWN BUT NO DOWNTOWN.

YOU CALL FREDERICTON "FREDDY BEACH" BUT YOU'RE NOT COMPLETELY SURE WHY YOU DO IT.

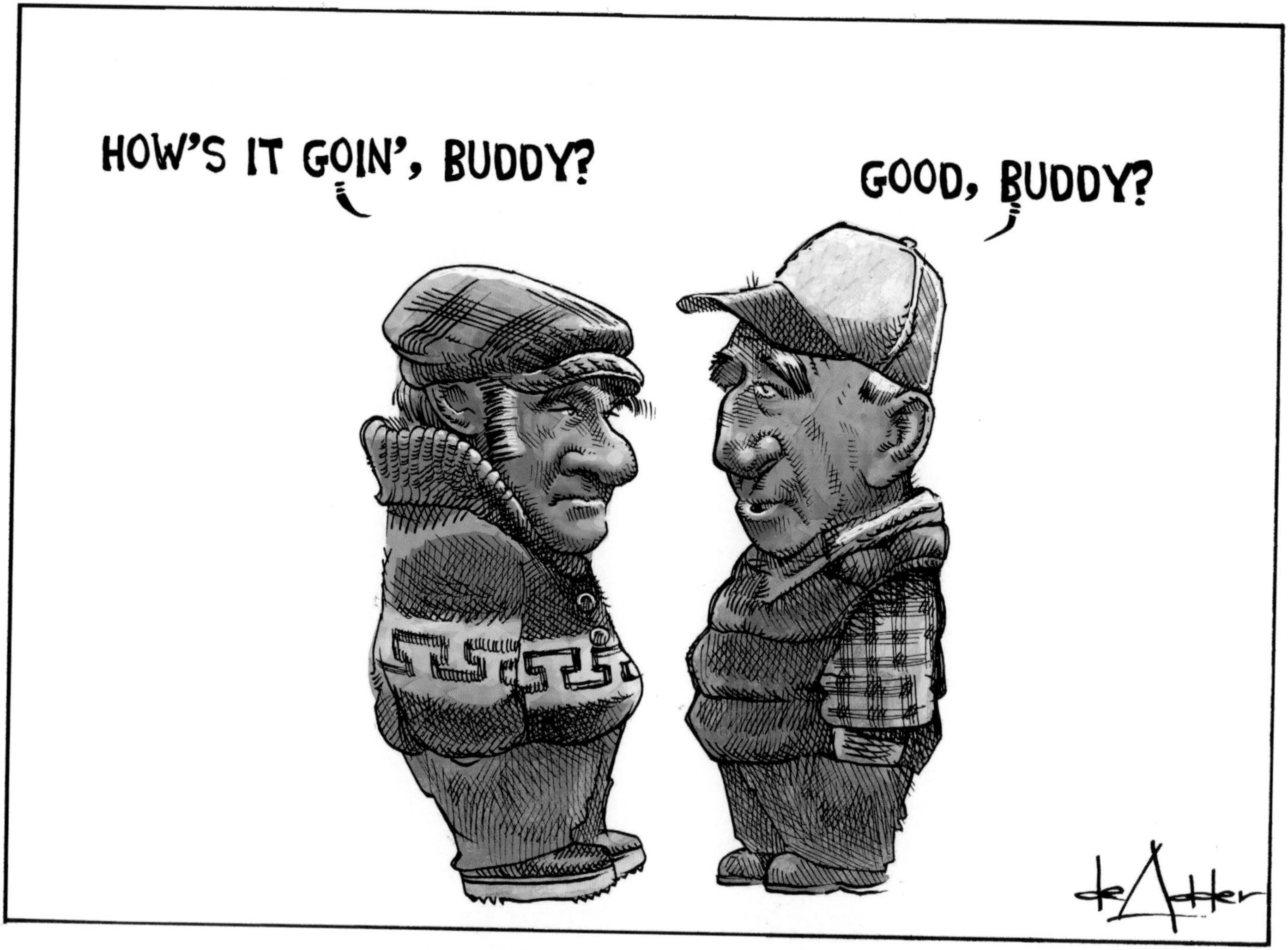
HOW'S IT GOIN', BUDDY?
GOOD, BUDDY?
de Adder

EVERYBODY IS BUDDY.

NOBODY CARES ABOUT THE TIME
YOU WENT TO WOODSTOCK.

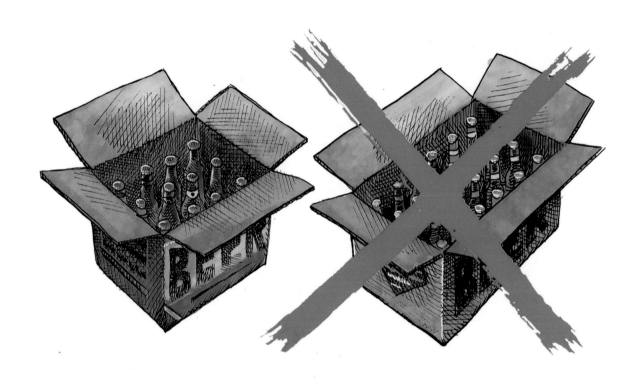

A "CASE" IS 12 BEER, NOT 24.

MAY

AND A "TWO FOUR" IS 24 BEER OR
A LONG WEEKEND IN MAY.

RIGHT ON MEANS THE SAME THING IN FRENCH
AS IT DOES IN ENGLISH.

YOU NEVER WON A MOOSE LICENCE, BUT YOU KNOW
PEOPLE WHO SEEM TO GET DRAWN EVERY YEAR.

YOU WENT ON A LONG DRIVE TO SEE AN OLD SOW.

TO CHILL YOUR BEER YOU ONLY NEED
TO PUT THEM ON THE DECK.

YOU REMEMBER DON MESSER'S JUBILEE.

YOU'RE AN EXPERT IN FINDING GREAT FISH AND CHIPS.

YOU KNOW THE PEI TOURISM NUMBER, BUT YOU DON'T KNOW THE ONE FOR NEW BRUNSWICK.

YOU HAVE A LIMO THAT'S FORTY FEET LONG.

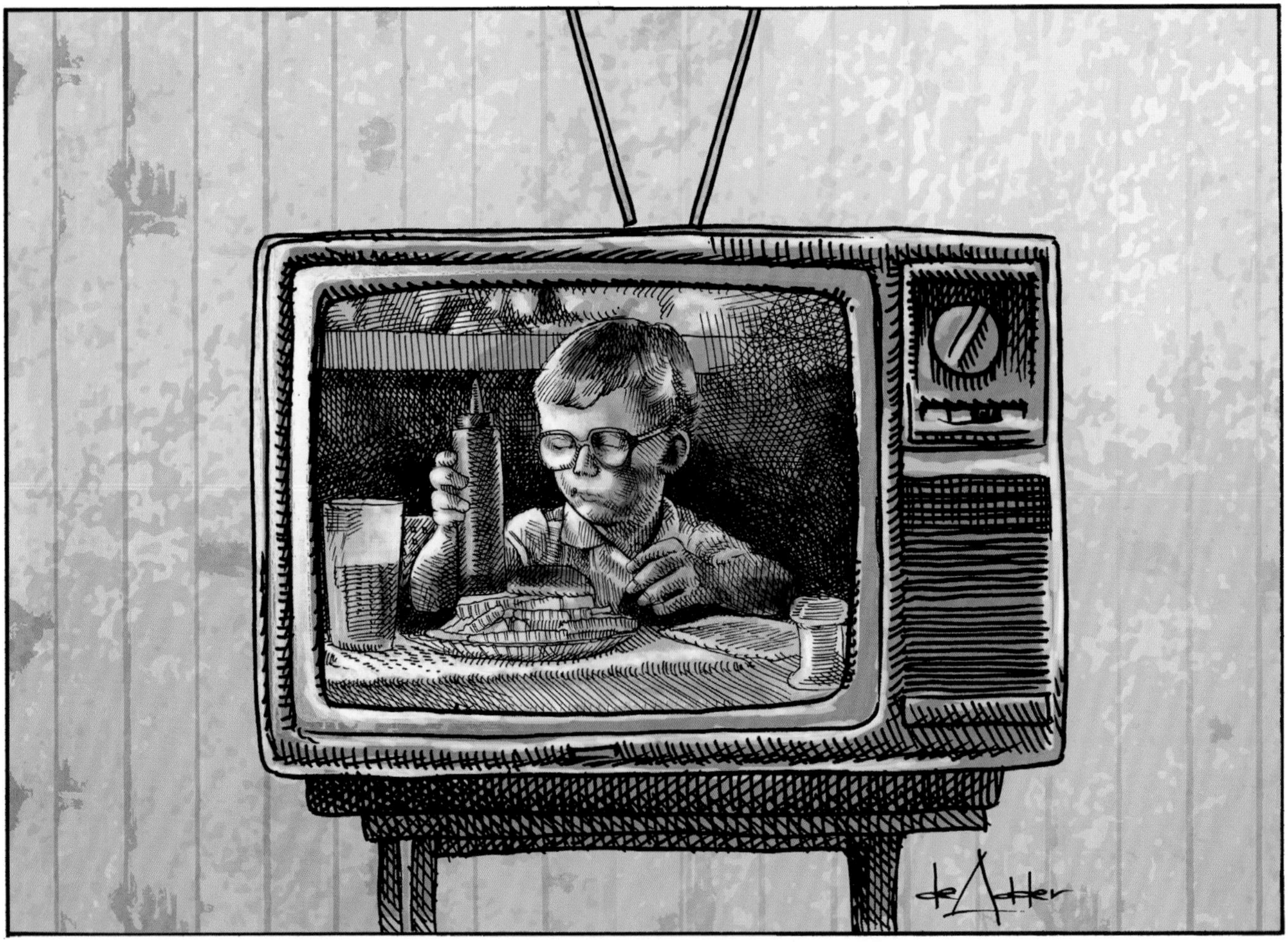

YOU REMEMBER JAY.

YOU REMEMBER WHEN THE ONLY THING ON TELEVISION WAS DICK STACEY'S COUNTRY JAMBOREE.

YOU KNOW THIS GUY WAS SO IMPORTANT,
THEY NAMED A MALL AFTER HIM.

YOU REMEMBER THE MONCTON FLYING SAUCER.

YOU STILL CALL THE CONFEDERATION BRIDGE
THE "FIXED LINK."

YOU KNOW A COMMUNITY THAT ONLY
EXISTS IN THE WINTER MONTHS.

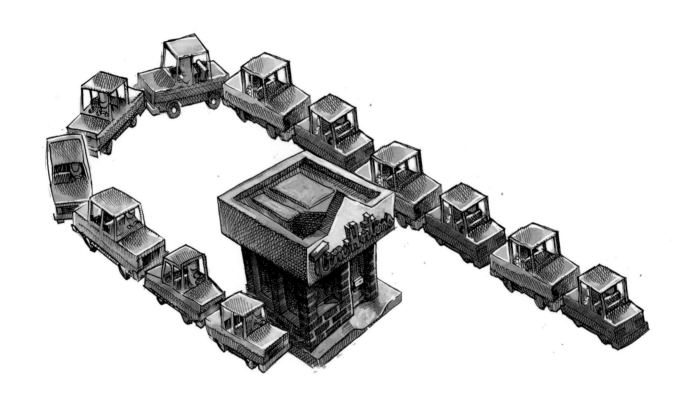

YOU HATE WAITING IN LINE AT THE BANK,
BUT WILL WAIT ALL DAY FOR A COFFEE.

DID YOU HEAR THE WEATHER REPORT FOR THE ST. JOHN RIVER AREA?"

EVERY YEAR YOU'RE WORRIED ABOUT FLOODING.

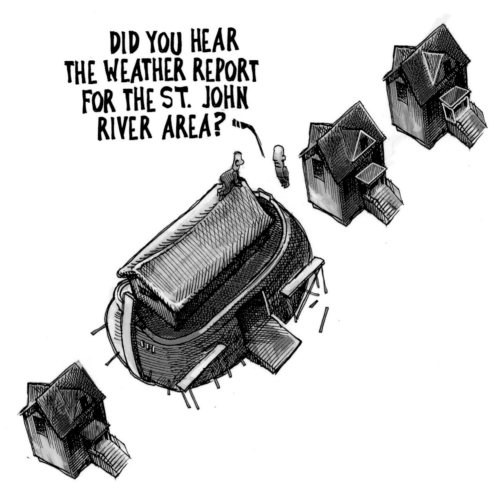

YOU REMEMBER CONSTABLES FABRICE GEVAUDAN,
DAVE ROSS AND DOUGLAS LARCHE.

YOU LOST FRIENDS AT YPRES, LIRI VALLEY AND THE SCHELDT.

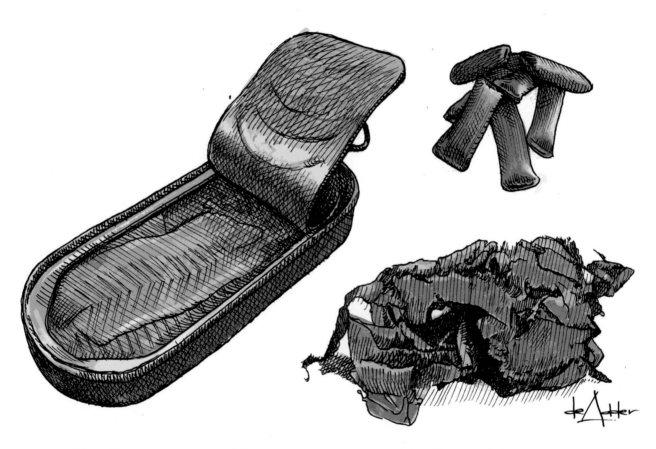

YOUR DIET CONSISTS OF KIPPER SNACKS,
CHICKEN BONES AND DULSE.

A SUNDAY DRIVE DOESN'T NECESSARILY
MEAN YOU'RE GOING TO CHURCH.

DEPENDING ON YOUR AGE, NEW BRUNSWICKER DONALD SUTHERLAND WAS EITHER THE ACTOR WHO PLAYED HAWKEYE IN THE ORIGINAL MASH OR THE ACTOR WHO PLAYED PRESIDENT SNOW IN THE HUNGER GAMES.

YOU KNOW ONE OF THE TRAILER PARK BOYS
IS FROM NEW BRUNSWICK.

YOU LIVE IN THE ONLY PROVINCE IN WHICH YOUR PREMIER WAS
CHARGED WITH THE CRIMINAL POSSESSION OF MARIJUANA.

WILLIE O'REE

YOU'RE PROUD THAT THE FIRST BLACK PLAYER
IN THE NHL CAME FROM NEW BRUNSWICK.

IN THE WINTER YOU SAVE HOURS OFF YOUR COMMUTE
BY TAKING THE HILLBILLY HIGHWAY.

YOUR FAVOURITE SHIRT IS FROM FRENCHYS.

YOU KNOW THE FIRST THREE INGREDIENTS OF TOURTIÈRE ARE MEAT, MEAT AND MEAT.

THE BEST FRIED CLAMS IN THE WORLD
COME FROM NEW BRUNSWICK.

YOU GAVE THE RIGHT OF WAY
TO A RIGHT WHALE.

YOU THOUGHT YOU HEARD THE DUNGARVON WHOOPER.

YOU KNOW TWO VERY IMPORTANT FOLK LEGENDS
WERE ORIGINALLY FROM NEW BRUNSWICK.

YOU TOOK A WALKING BRIDGE TO THE LAND OF THE WASHERWOMEN.

ONCE A YEAR YOU GIVE YOUR THUMBS
A WORKOUT.

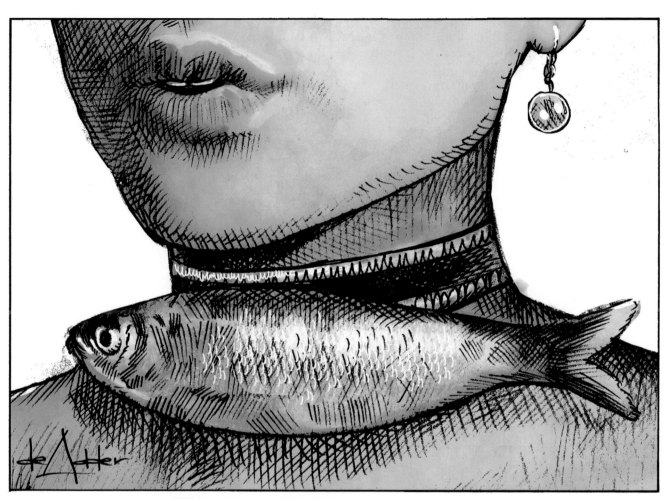

YOU'RE NOT REALLY SURE WHAT
A HERRING CHOKER REFERS TO.

YOU STOP DEAD TO LET JAYWALKERS CROSS THE ROAD.

WHEN GIVING DIRECTIONS YOU USE UP AND DOWN
INSTEAD OF NORTH AND SOUTH.

YOU DON'T KNOW WHAT THESE ARE FOR.

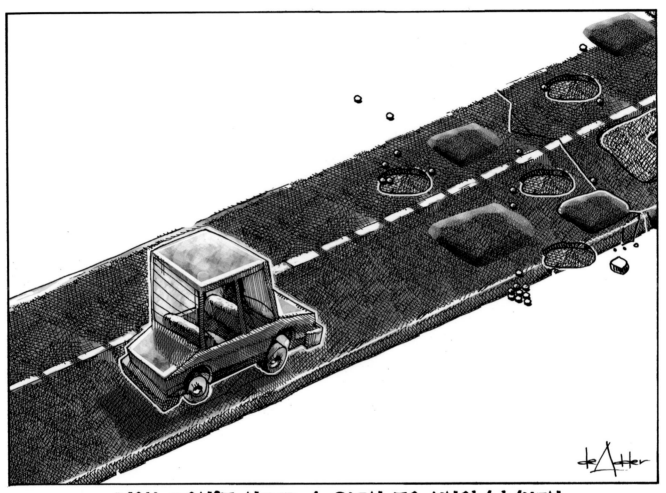

YOU DON'T NEED A SIGN TO KNOW WHEN
YOU'VE CROSSED THE BORDER INTO NEW BRUNSWICK.

YOU REMEMBER BUYING FRENCH FRIES FROM A TRUCK.

YOU KNOW WHO KILLER KARL KRUPP, LEO BURKE AND BIG STEPHEN PETITPAS ARE.

YOU CALL THE BORDER WITH MAINE "ACROSS THE LINES."

THERE'S A SEPARATE PARKING LOT FOR SNOWMOBILES.

MOUNT ALLISON ALWAYS SEEMS TO TOP MACLEAN'S UNIVERSITY RANKING.

EVERY JUNE 6TH, YOU'RE REMINDED WHAT THE
NORTH SHORE NEW BRUNSWICK REGIMENT DID ON D-DAY.

TO THIS DAY, YOU STILL DON'T KNOW WHAT "BE...IN THIS PLACE" MEANS.

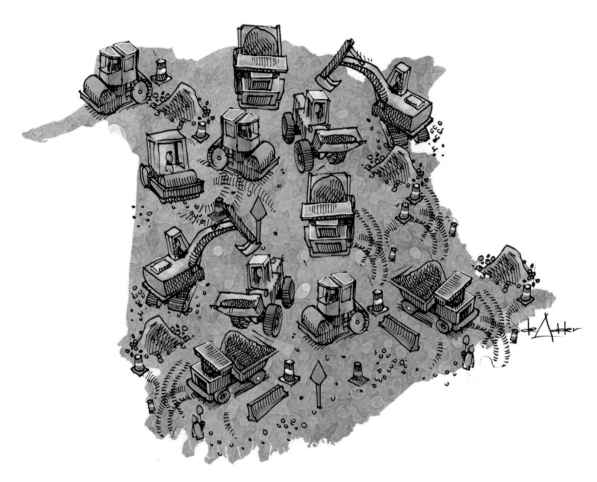

SUMMER DRIVING CAN BE AS
SLOW AS WINTER DRIVING.

YOU KNOW LORD BEAVERBROOK IS IMPORTANT
BUT YOU'RE NOT COMPLETELY SURE WHY.

YOU FLOATED DOWN THE POLLETT RIVER ON
A HOMEMADE RAFT.

YOU SAW AN ATTRACTION AT MAGNETIC HILL.

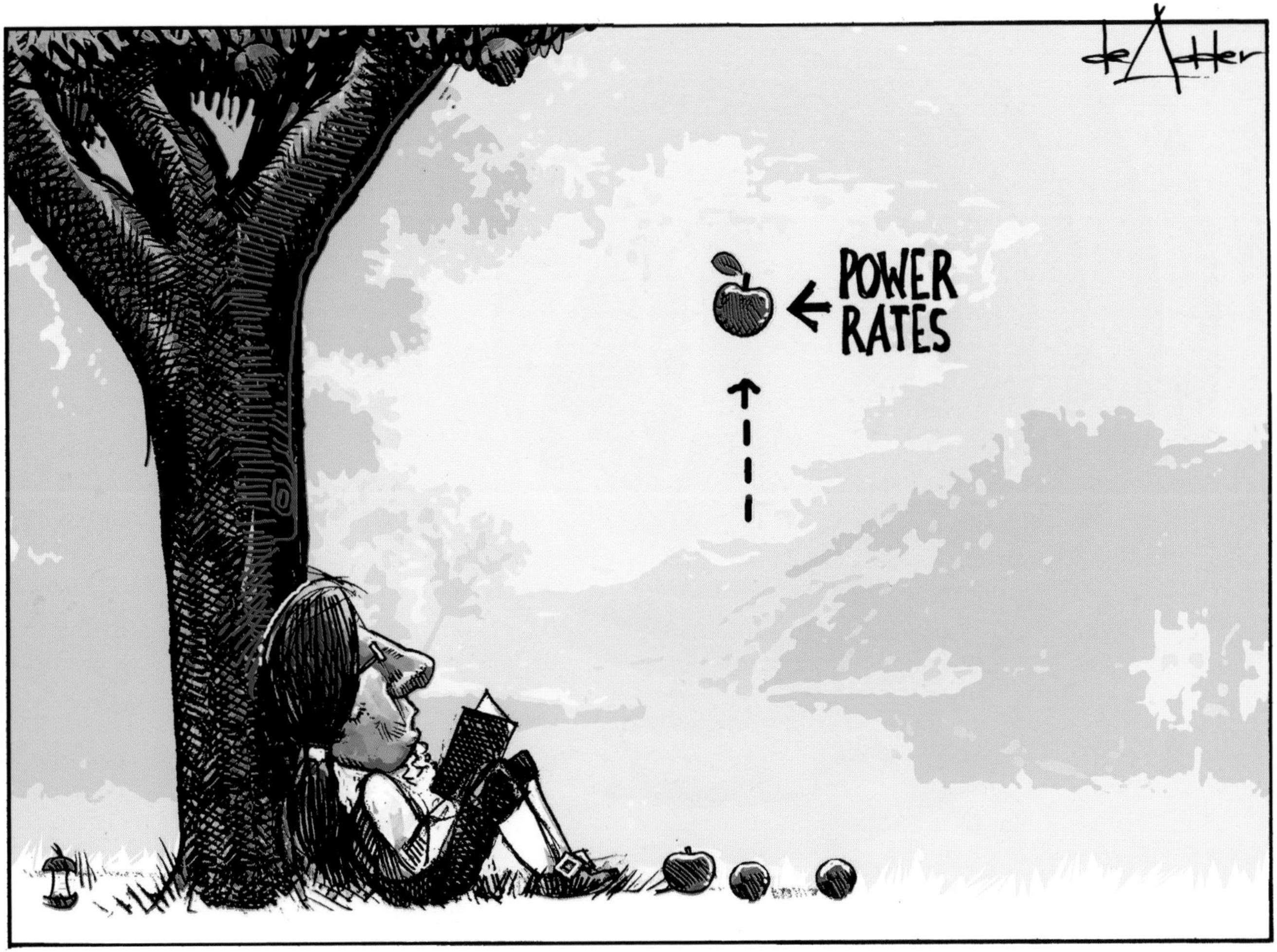
POWER RATES

THERE'S ONE EXCEPTION TO THE LAW OF GRAVITY.

YOU KNOW THE ICE CREAM CONE
WAS INVENTED IN NEW BRUNSWICK.

YOU'RE SPOILED BY WARM OCEAN TEMPERATURES.

YOU CAN VISIT AN ENGLISH AND A FRENCH HISTORIC VILLAGE.

YOU KNOW REVERSING FALLS ARE ACTUALLY RAPIDS.

PURCHASING CURLY FRIES IS CONSIDERED BUYING LOCAL.

IF YOU REMEMBER ANYTHING FROM STUDYING CHARLES G.D. ROBERTS IN HIGH SCHOOL, IT IS THAT HE'S FROM NEW BRUNSWICK.

YOU REMEMBER THE OLD DAYS WHEN YOU USED TO
CALL THE TIDAL BORE THE "TOTAL BORE."

A VACATION MEANS YOU'RE
GOING TO MONCTON.

YOU'VE HAD YOUR PICTURE TAKEN
WITH A WELL-DRESSED POTATO.

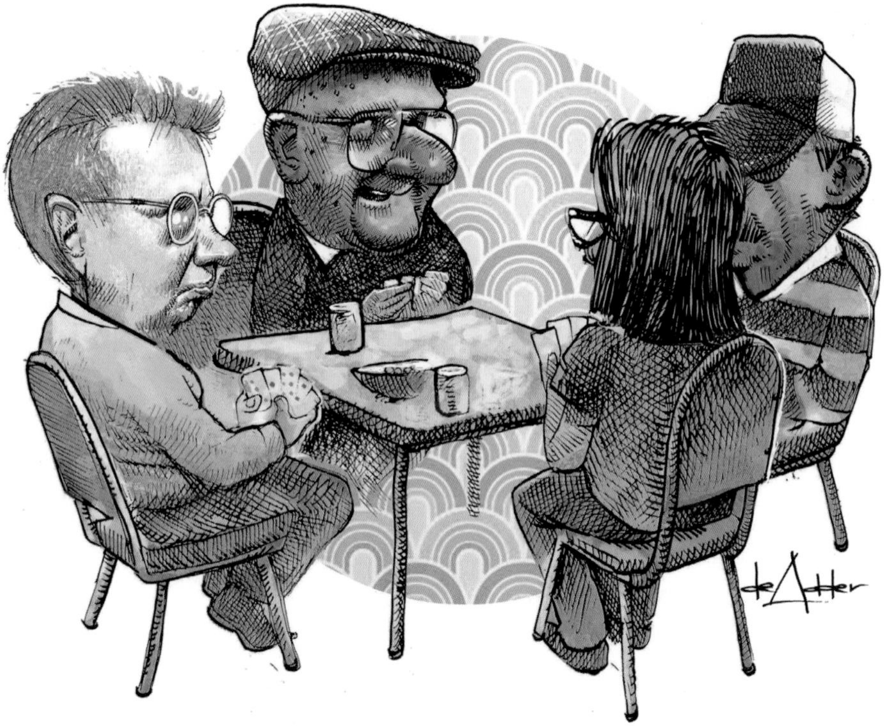
deAdder

YOU PLAY 200.

YOU HAVE "CALL CENTRE" ON YOUR RÉSUMÉ.

YOU REMEMBER WHEN THERE WERE ONLY THREE CHANNELS:
THE ENGLISH CHANNEL, THE FRENCH CHANNEL
AND THE FUZZY CHANNEL.

YOU CONSIDER THIS SIGN TO BE A SUGGESTION.

YOU CAN BUY A LOBSTER BOAT ON KIJIJI.

YOU DIDN'T LEAVE THE HIGHWAY.

IF WINTER SEEMS TOO LONG.

YOU SEE EVERY TYPE OF WEATHER
IN 15 MINUTE INTERVALS.